Dwyane Wade

by John Smallwood

SCHOLASTIC INC.

New York Toronto London Auckland Sydney
Mexico City New Delhi Hong Kong Buenos Aires

PHOTO CREDITS

All photos are © NBA/Getty Images
Front cover: Doug Benc
Back cover: Andrew D. Bernstein

Interiors:
(4, 7) Eliot J. Schechter; (5) Rocky Widner; (8, 28) Andrew D. Bernstein;
(9) Fernando Medina; (10) David Sherman; (13, 15) Jonathan Daniel;
(14, 16, 18) Victor Baldizon; (19, 31) Issac Baldizon; (20) Stuart Hannagan;
(21) Jim McIsaac; (22) Nathaniel S. Butler; (23) Ronald Martinez; (24) Glenn James;
(26) Jesse D. Garrabrant; (27) Stephen Dunn

ISBN-13: 978-0-439-91237-2
ISBN-10: 0-439-91237-7

Copyright © 2007 by NBA Properties, Inc.
All rights reserved. Published by Scholastic Inc.

SCHOLASTIC and associated logos are trademarks
and/or registered trademarks of Scholastic Inc.

12 11 10 9 8 7 6 5 4 3 2 1   7 8 9 10 11/0

Printed in the U.S.A.
First printing, February 2007
Book Design: Kim Brown and Henry Ng

Contents

Chapter 1 — Meet Dwyane Wade 5

Chapter 2 — Growing Up 11

Chapter 3 — From 5 to No. 1 17

Chapter 4 — Superman Arrives 21

Chapter 5 — Flash to the Future 25

Meet Dwyane Wade

In a different NBA draft, Dwyane Wade probably would have received the full attention he deserved.

But in 2003, all of the talk was about high school sensation LeBron James, who was already being called the next Michael Jordan.

In addition, there was Syracuse University freshman Carmelo Anthony, who led the Orange to the NCAA Championship, and Darko Milicic, the mysterious kid from Europe who everyone was excited about.

All Dwyane had done was lead Marquette University to the 2003 NCAA Final Four, average 21.5 points and 4.4 assists, be named Conference USA Player of the Year, and become First Team All-America!

Still there wasn't a lot of talk about Dwyane before the draft. He understood, but that didn't mean he accepted what people weren't saying about him.

On draft night, Dwyane sat patiently in the family area at Madison Square Garden with his wife, Siohvaughn, and their son, Zaire. He wouldn't wait that long.

LeBron was picked first by the Cleveland Cavaliers. Darko was picked second by the Detroit Pistons, and Carmelo went third to the Denver Nuggets.

Then the Toronto Raptors selected Chris Bosh, a forward from Georgia Tech, with the fourth pick.

"With the fifth pick in the 2003 NBA Draft," NBA commissioner David Stern said, "the Miami Heat select Dwyane Wade, guard from Marquette University."

Dwyane hugged his wife and son and then walked to the stage to shake hands with the commissioner and receive a baseball hat with the logo of the Miami Heat.

His dream had come true. He was officially an NBA player.

"No, actually, I was wide open," Dwyane, a native of Illinois, said when asked if he knew Miami was the team for him. "There was a lot of talk at the time that Chicago was going to pick me at seven, and I didn't know what would happen.

"It's a good thing because I didn't want to know. I wanted it to be a surprise, and it was. It was a big surprise."

Maybe it was not as big of a surprise as Dwyane believed.

At that time, Pat Riley was the coach and president of the Miami Heat. When he was coach of the Los Angeles Lakers, he had won four NBA Championships with Hall of Fame guard Earvin "Magic" Johnson. Because of Magic, Pat Riley knew how important a guard with great talent and leadership skills could be. He saw those things in Dwyane.

"To sum up the evening, at least for us, we feel like we have one of the best players in the draft, if not the best," Pat Riley said after he drafted Dwyane. "We are excited about him and feel like he is going to be a great asset and a great player for us. He is a complete player who is going to get better."

Nobody knew how right Pat Riley was.

After just three seasons, Dwyane has become one of the best players in the NBA.

As a rookie, he averaged 16.2 points, 4.5 assists, and had 247 rebounds. The 6-foot-4 guard helped lead Miami to the playoffs for the first time in two seasons and was an NBA All-Rookie First Team selection.

Dwyane was so impressive during his first season that he was selected as a member of the 2004 United States Olympic Team, which would win a bronze medal at the Athens games.

That summer, the Heat also made a huge move by getting All-Star center Shaquille O'Neal from the Los Angeles Lakers.

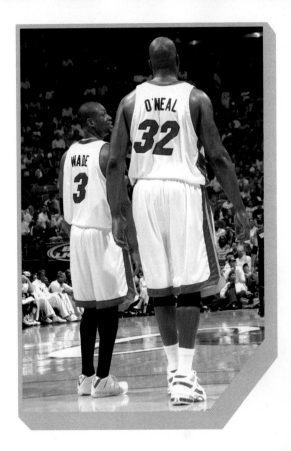

Having a superstar for a teammate didn't hurt Dwyane. In fact, it made him a better player.

Dwyane's speed and quickness earned him the nickname "Flash" from his teammate Shaq.

He was named to his first NBA All-Star Team and was voted All-NBA Second Team and NBA All-Defensive Second Team.

It became clear to everyone that the Heat's future would be hot with Dwyane on the team.

In 2006, Dwyane led the Heat to the NBA Finals for the first time in the team's 18-year history.

Growing Up

Dwyane Tyrone Wade, Jr., was born on January 17, 1982, on the South Side of Chicago, Illinois.

His early life was not easy.

His parents divorced soon after he was born and Dwyane lived with his mother, Jolinda, and older sister, Tragil, in a crime-ridden neighborhood.

"I grew up seeing all of it," Dwyane said. "People selling, people using drugs, guns, shootings."

It was the type of place where a child like Dwyane could have easily gone down the wrong path and ended up getting into all kinds of trouble.

But Dwyane had a guardian angel in Tragil.

Tragil was an honor student at Englewood High School, and she saw the dangers that could ruin her brother's life. She was determined not to let him fall in with a bad crowd or get into trouble.

"My main challenge in trying to keep [Dwyane] safe was protecting him from the negative peer pressure from other boys," Tragil once told the *Chicago Sun Times* in a story about her brother. "I had to keep letting him know that he was different. He did not have to get into the trouble they were getting into."

Tragil helped teach Dwyane how to read and write. She helped him with his homework. She took him to museums. She made sure he went to church and stayed out of trouble.

"She pretty much raised me," Dwyane said of Tragil. "She was the biggest influence in keeping me out of trouble and keeping me focused to grow up and become a good person and a hard worker.

"No matter what problem I ever had, she was always there for me, helping me to do the right thing."

When Dwyane was nine years old, Tragil, who was only thirteen at the time, made the decision to get her brother out of the neighborhood where they were living.

One day, Tragil told Dwyane that she was taking him to see a movie, but instead, she took him to the suburbs of Chicago to live with his father, Dwyane, Sr.

It was while living in Robbins, Illinois, that Dwyane first started playing basketball. Robbins was also where he met another important person in his life, his future wife Siohvaughn.

Dwyane attended Richards High School in Oak Lawn, Illinois. Although Dwyane was a great player at Richards, not many colleges recruited him. He ended up attending Marquette University in Milwaukee, Wisconsin.

"Marquette was the biggest school that recruited me," Dwyane said. "I was happy to go to Marquette."

But it wasn't easy.

Marquette coach Tom Crean knew it would take a lot of practice for the Golden Eagles to compete in Conference USA with big-name schools like Cincinnati, DePaul, Louisville, and Memphis. He required that his players work very hard.

"At the time, my freshman year, I was thinking it isn't worth

it," Dwyane said of the hard practices. "But then I found myself getting better. We started winning. We made the NCAA Tournament and then it was like all this work is what we need."

Dwyane also married his high school sweetheart, Siohvaughn, while he was at Marquette and they had a son, Zaire.

Being a husband, a father, a student, and a star basketball player was a lot of work for Dwyane, but he was determined to be the best at all of them.

During his junior year at Marquette, the Golden Eagles made it to the Final Four of the 2003 NCAA Tournament.

In one memorable tournament victory over Kentucky, Dwyane became the third player ever to record a triple-double in NCAA tournament history, by totaling 29 points, 11 rebounds, and 11 assists.

Although Marquette lost in the Final Four to Kansas, Dwyane decided that with a family to take

care of, he should enter the NBA draft after just two seasons at Marquette.

"Something inside of me wanted to go back," Dwyane said, "but I had to do the best thing for me and my family."

From 5 to No. 1

Everybody wanted the first pick in the 2003 NBA Draft because that meant getting high school sensation LeBron James.

But when it was all over, the Miami Heat were very happy to have had the fifth pick, because it meant they got Dwyane.

The Heat had been a powerful team in the Eastern Conference for most of the 1990s, but when star center Alonzo Mourning had to miss significant time because of a serious illness, Miami missed the playoffs for two straight seasons. Drafting Dwyane was the first step in the rebuilding process.

Dwyane had his ability to adapt tested immediately as the Heat moved him from shooting to point guard.

"It was a big adjustment for me, going to the point guard," said Dwyane, who had a team-high 18 points in his first NBA game. "I was trying to be

the point guard, but then, I'm
a scorer.

"But this is what the Miami
Heat drafted me for, so that's
what I'm going to do. I'll
always be a point guard with
the mentality of a scorer, but
most of my mentality is to
make plays. I think that's the
big thing."

Dwyane started 56 of 61
games his first season. It
would have been more, but
he missed 21 games due to injury.

He earned Eastern Conference Player of the
Week honors on February 23, 2004, becoming
the first Heat rookie ever to earn that award.

Dwyane was All-Rookie First Team and finished
third in the Rookie of the Year race behind LeBron
James and Carmelo Anthony.

But the most important thing to Dwyane, who
averaged 16.2 points and 4.5 assists, was that
Miami finished a surprising 42–40 and made the
playoffs.

Dwyane started all 13 playoff games for
Miami and averaged 18 points, 5.6 assists, and
4.0 rebounds.

In his first playoff game, Dwyane hit the winning shot with 1.3 seconds left as the Heat beat the New Orleans Hornets 81–79.

In the series victory, Dwyane also broke a tie with a three-pointer in the final minute that put

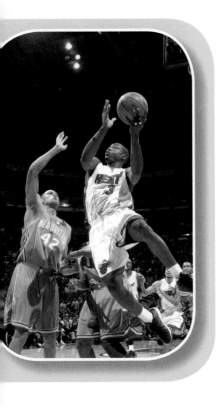

Miami up for good in Game 5. He went on to set a Heat rookie record with 27 points in the series, clinching Game 6.

Dwyane's four 20-point games were the most by an NBA rookie in a playoff series since Arvydas Sabonis had four 20-point games for Portland in 1996.

Miami lost in the Eastern Conference Semifinals to the Indiana Pacers, but Dwyane had three more 20-point games in that seven-game series.

"My will is to always be better and better," Dwyane said. "I've got to want to be the best."

Superman Arrives

T he summer of 2004 was a significant one in Dwyane's career.

He represented the United States in the Olympics in Athens, Greece, averaging 7.3 points and 2.4 assists to help the team win the bronze medal.

But the big change for Dwyane and the Heat had come on July 14, when Miami acquired center Shaquille O'Neal from the Los Angeles Lakers in a trade for Lamar Odom, Caron Butler, Brian Grant, and a first-round draft pick.

Shaq had led the Lakers to three straight NBA titles and promised to bring a championship to Miami.

Dwyane and Shaq brought out the best in each other.

With Dwyane making sure he stayed involved, Shaquille averaged 22.9 points and shot a career-high 60.1 percent from the floor.

"[Dwyane] is a humble kid," Shaq said. "He works hard and really cares about getting his teammates involved and making them better."

Playing with the superstar big man, Dwyane took his game to another level.

In 77 games, Dwyane led the Heat in scoring (24.1 points a game), assists (6.8), and steals (1.57). He tied a franchise record by scoring at least 20 points in 12 straight games.

He scored 14 in his first All-Star game and was named second team All-NBA and second team All-Defense. He was the Eastern Conference Player of the Month for December.

With Dwyane and Shaquille tearing up the

competition, Miami finished 59–23, the best record in the Eastern Conference.

The Heat was favored to go to the NBA Finals, but a deep bruise in his right thigh hampered Shaquille.

Dwyane picked up the load by averaging 26.3 points and 8.8 assists in a first-round sweep of New Jersey. He then averaged 31.0 points, 8.0 assists, and 7.0 rebounds in a semifinal victory over Washington.

In the Eastern Conference Finals, Miami was tied 2–2 with Detroit when Dwyane strained his right rib muscle in the third quarter of Game 5.

The Heat won, but the injury caused Dwyane to miss Game 6, which the Pistons won to set up a decisive Game 7 in Miami.

Dwyane played but he was clearly hurt.

He had 20 points and 4 assists, but the Pistons eliminated the Heat with an 88–82 victory.

Flash to the Future

During the 2005–2006 season, Dwyane continued to be recognized as one of the top players in the NBA.

He was voted as a starter to the All-Star Game for the first time and scored the game-winning basket in Houston.

Dwyane was again named All-NBA Second Team and he was selected as one of the core players for the United States National Team that competed in the 2006 FIBA World Championship in Japan and will try to win gold at the 2008 Olympics in Beijing, China.

That was a significant personal milestone, but the most important thing to Dwyane has always been the success of his team.

After losing the Eastern Conference Finals in 2005, the pressure was on the Heat to make the NBA Finals in 2006.

Pat Riley changed the roster and returned to coach the team again.

Dwyane had an incredible season, averaging 27.2 points, 6.7 assists, and 5.7 rebounds as Miami made the playoffs for the third straight season.

He was even better in the playoffs.

He averaged 24.7 points and 7.2 assists as Miami beat the Chicago Bulls in the first round. He averaged 27.6 points and 6.6 assists as the Heat beat the New Jersey Nets in the Eastern Conference Semifinals.

But Dwyane had saved his best for the Eastern Conference Finals rematch with Detroit.

Through the first five games, Dwyane averaged 29.2 points and 4.6 assists as Miami took a 3–2 lead in the series.

But on the morning of Game 6, Dwyane woke up with a severe case of the flu. He was in the hospital from 8 a.m. until 3 p.m.

When he got to the AmericanAirlines Arena before the biggest game in Miami Heat history, no one was sure if he would be able to play. But Dwyane was not going to miss this game.

"I was feeling a little weak, but I was still here mentally," Dwyane said. "I really wasn't worried."

Dwyane scored 14 points and had 10 assists as Miami beat the Pistons to move on to the NBA Finals.

In the finals, Dwyane was awarded the Most Valuable Player award. He was virtually unstoppable, scoring at will. His scoring average of 34.7 points was the third highest for a player in his first NBA Finals.

After the Dallas Mavericks won the first two games, Dwyane averaged 40.3 points to lead Miami to wins in the next three. In the championship-clinching Game 6 in Dallas, Dwyane had 36 points, 10 rebounds, 5 assists, and 4 steals.

When asked what he is the most proud of, Dwyane answered, "Being in the playoffs. Being known as a winner in my short career so far."

And of course, the Heat's winning player got to lead the victory parade in an all-day celebration at Disney World.

READ TO ACHIEVE

Read to Achieve is the NBA's year-round, league-wide initiative that promotes the value of reading and online literacy and encourages families and adults to read regularly with young children. With the support of longtime national partners such as Reading Is Fundamental and Scholastic Inc., the NBA and its teams will create Read to Achieve Reading and Learning Centers throughout North America in an effort to provide access to reading materials and technology to young people everywhere. The NBA has also formed national and local All-Star Reading Teams comprised of current and former NBA, WNBA and NBDL players and other members of the NBA family, who promote the value of reading through in-arena events, public service announcements, and school and community appearances. The NBA, WNBA and NBDL and its teams and players, are committed to developing in children a lifelong love for reading.

For more information, log on to:

 **NBA.COM**